Draw a Portrait of a Girl in 21 Days

Christopher Shellhammer

Website and contact info:
www.christophershellhammergallery.com

First edition.
ISBN: 978-1-387-75597-4

Printed in U.S.A.

Contents

It Really Takes Two

It takes two to make a territory,
it takes two make a relationship,
it takes two to make a society,
it takes two make an audience,
otherwise, there is no need.

Now it takes two,
you and me,
I write and paint you a picture,
you read and enjoy the pleasure.

Introduction

Here is the portrait drawing lesson book in step by step, "Draw a Portrait of a Girl in 21 Days," in quarter view pose, and it is the program of learning to draw for the beginner to advanced level. In this book explains how and what I use to make a beautiful portrait in drawing and painting alike. I have taught these skills on university or college's level, but anyone at any age can learn this specialized skills and tools I have developed over the span of 40 years. It only requires a lot of patience and attention of an artist to pursue and learn these skills.

All in all, I will be revealing my hidden skills in all these years of how I make a portrait the natural way. Over the years, I have tried and experimented the various logical idea of how to measure a person's head from either photograph or life. I concluded that the methods I use is the best reasonable way for me to draw a portrait for drawing and painting alike. I will share it with you in this book. It may not fit or agree with everyone, but at least you will know how I did it to bring to a near perfect portrait naturally. I have picked up these methods by accident in my late teen days, and it had produced such a beautiful result over and over without much frustration or struggle.

There are several diagrams-worksheets included in this book for learning the easy way to draw from beginner to advanced level. An average of several weeks to a month to develop this skill in drawing this portrait and you can use this method to draw other portraits. Be sure to make several xerox copies of these diagrams-worksheets so you can practice as often as you want without using the actual diagrams-worksheets to save the book for later use.

First Chapter
The Portrait

On the next page, page 5 is a drawing of a portrait of a girl in quarter view in this project.

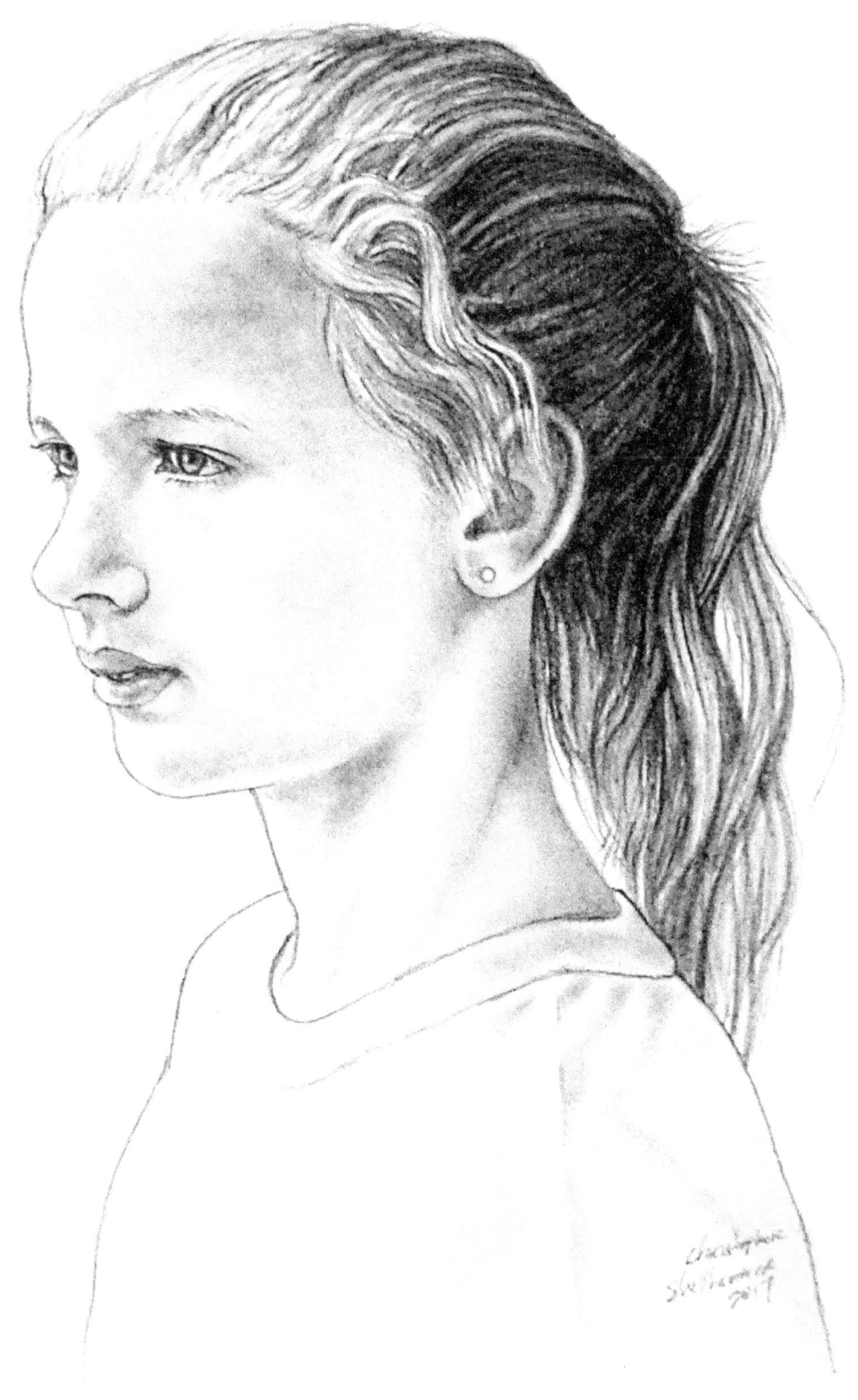

The following next page, on page 7 is a photograph of a girl that was used for this project.

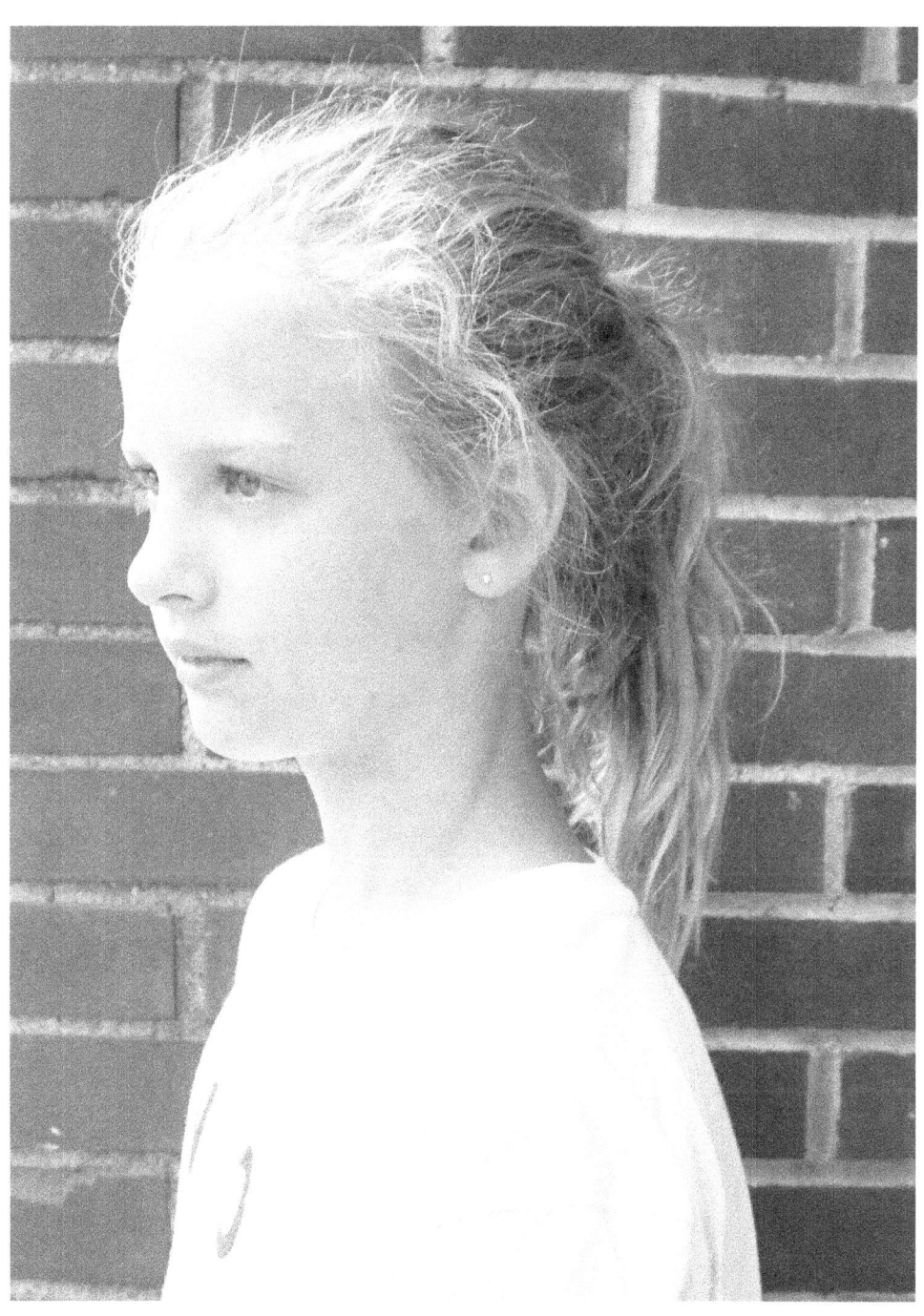

Second Chapter
The Tools

List of tools to keep it handy

1. Metal Compass and metal compass with pencil
2. Pencils, School no.2, B3, B4, B5 and B6
3. Cotton swabs
4. White tissues
5. Clay eraser kneadable
6. White eraser/architecture eraser
7. Hair spray (non-coloring and non-sticky) or Artist fixative (glossy only)
8. Bristol, 220g/m2 to 300g/m2 thick paper
9. Masking tape and Masonite board

Metal compass is an ideal use for all source of measurement for the portrait, landscape, still life and much more. You can measure it on the photograph or from life.

Pencils in different shade allow me to apply different lighting and shadows on the portrait and subject. Use all soft pencils or in B grade and the School no.2 will be the only hard pencil.

A cotton swab is a fantastic tool to smooth out shade or blending. It is what we called a gradation.

The white tissue is an excellent way of blending in lightly of the broad area of shade like the cheek of a portrait or the sky in the landscape drawing.

Clay eraser kneadable is a soft eraser to allow me to shape it in any form and to lighten the dark area of the shade without erasing it altogether.

The white eraser or architecture eraser is crucial so you can tell if it is clean before you erase the specific area of the drawing to prevent smudge. To clean the white eraser each time is to rub it lightly on tough linen-like blue jean or cloth.

Hairspray (non-coloring and non-sticky) or artist fixative spray in glossy only are the excellent use for preserving your work better than matte spray which does not hold up as well. And you can draw or erase again even after you finish your drawing. Be sure to spray lightly enough that it does not smudge. Try not to use more than one coat since it may start yellowing your beautiful drawing when it aged. You give one good coat spraying side to side and up and down evenly at one spray.

Bristol paper, I use it from a 9 x 12 inches pad or in a large sheet 22 x 30 inches and cut it up in 8.5 x 11 inches. The best paper in thickness is 220g/m2 and up. You can buy it in any art or office supply store.

Masking tape is an excellent way of holding down your drawing on a drawing board or masonite board. You can use a smooth hard masonite board and cut into a smaller size like 15 x 15 inches or larger to fit on your lap or your desk so you can move it around while you are drawing. You can use these board over and over again for years to come.

See the picture below of the tools that I use.
Bristol paper and masonite board is not included in the picture.

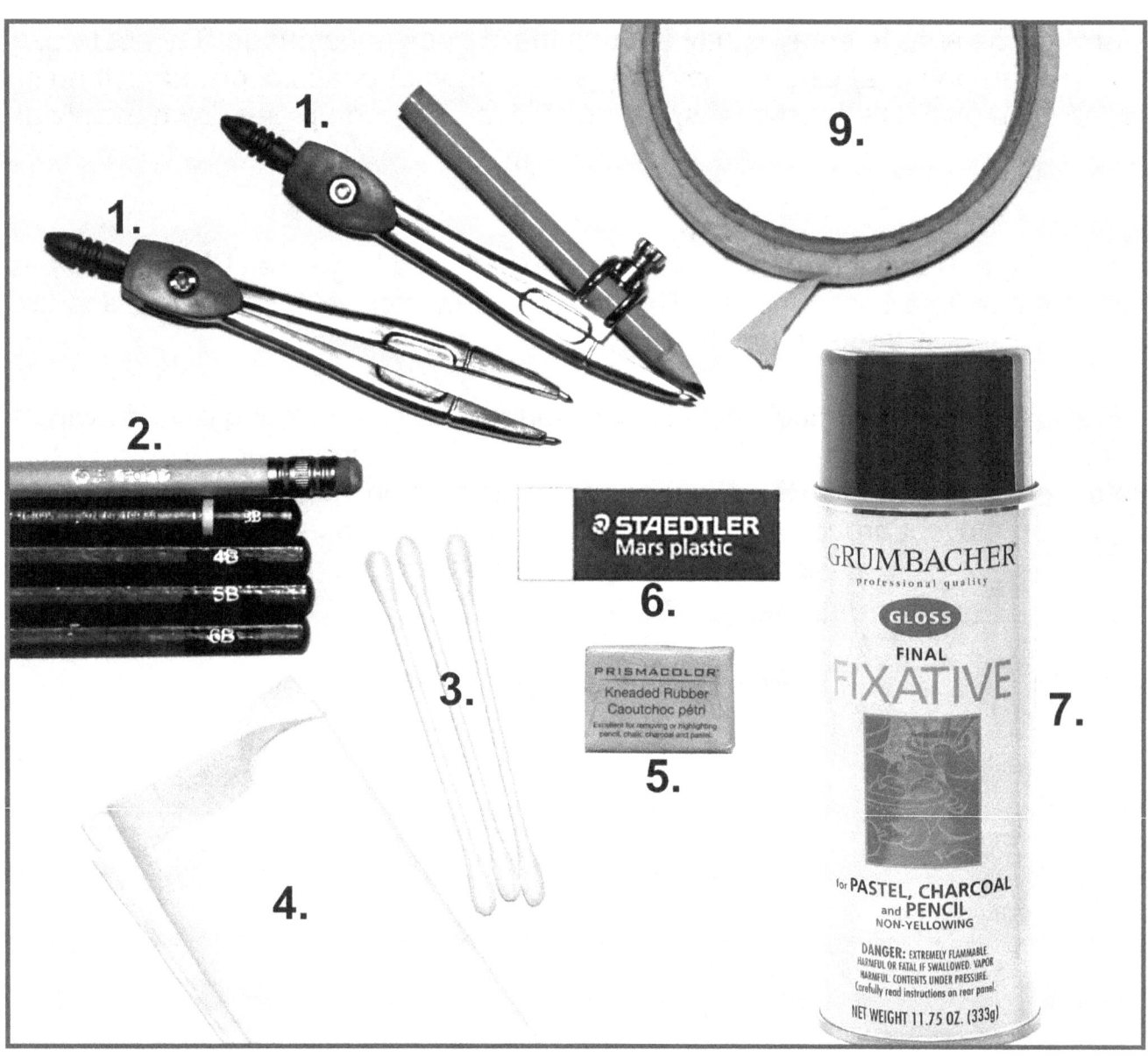

Third Chapter
The Methods

On the following pages, on page 15, 16 and 17. I am showing the three methods that I use for measuring the portrait with the free hand. I would use any body parts as a measurement. By using the compass (without the compass pencil for now), I usually use the measurement between the bottom of the nose to the top of the lips in the groove as a guide shown in photo A on page 15.

Another method is using the compass (without the compass pencil for now) from the bottom of the nose, underneath to the eyebrows in shown photo B on page 16.

Another method is using a School no. 2 pencil shown in photo C on page 17 which I use it when I person is sitting for a live portrait drawing, but this is for advanced level once you practice the A and B to become familiar with the mental measurement.

Bear in mind that each face is slightly different from one another in term of size. In this order, the measurement in the picture is for her face for the portrait drawing. You can do this from real life by having the person sitting still or do it from the photograph. It gets easier as time passes with many practices. It's ok to fail few or many times because that is how we learn to improve our skills by learning from our mistakes.

Photo A.

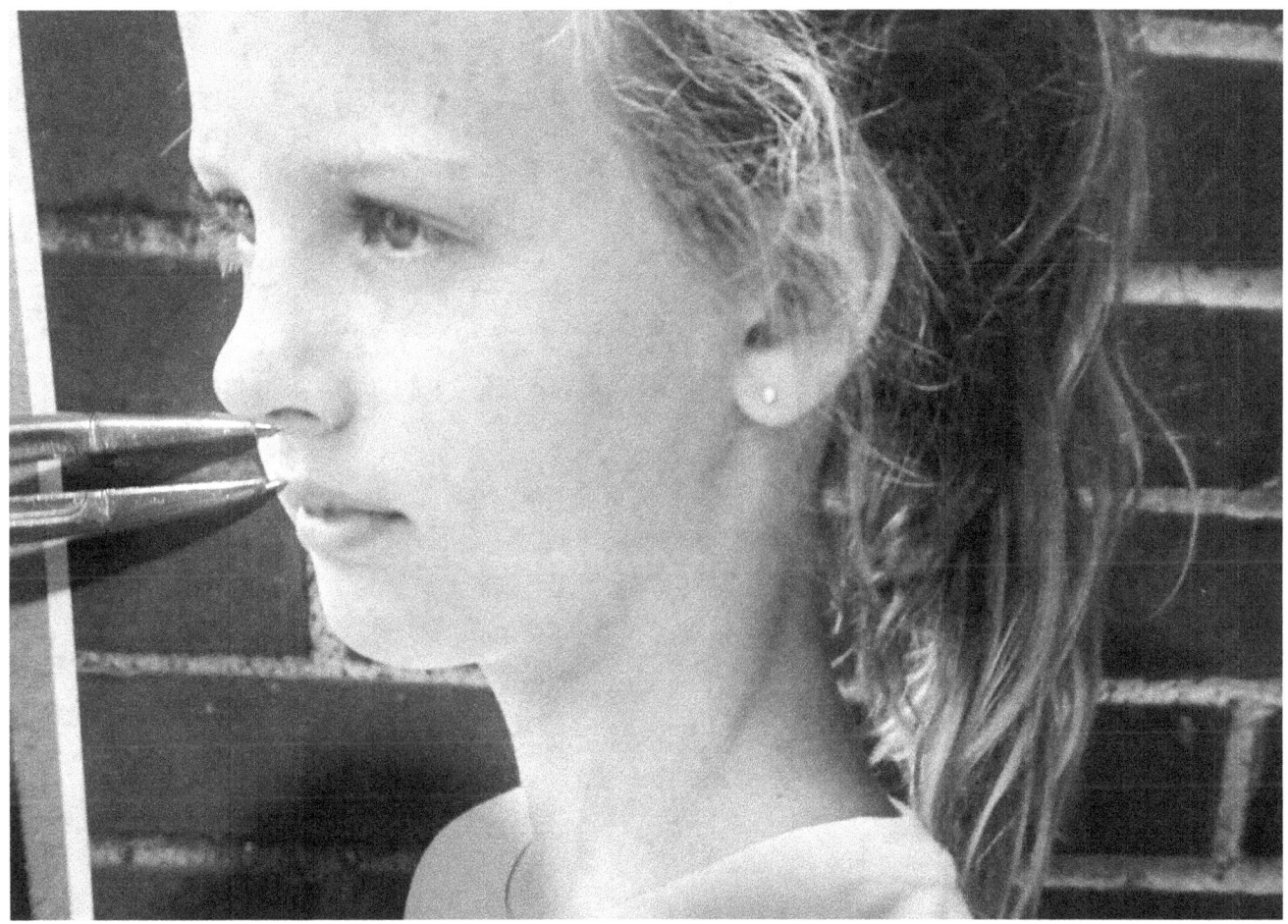

Photo B.

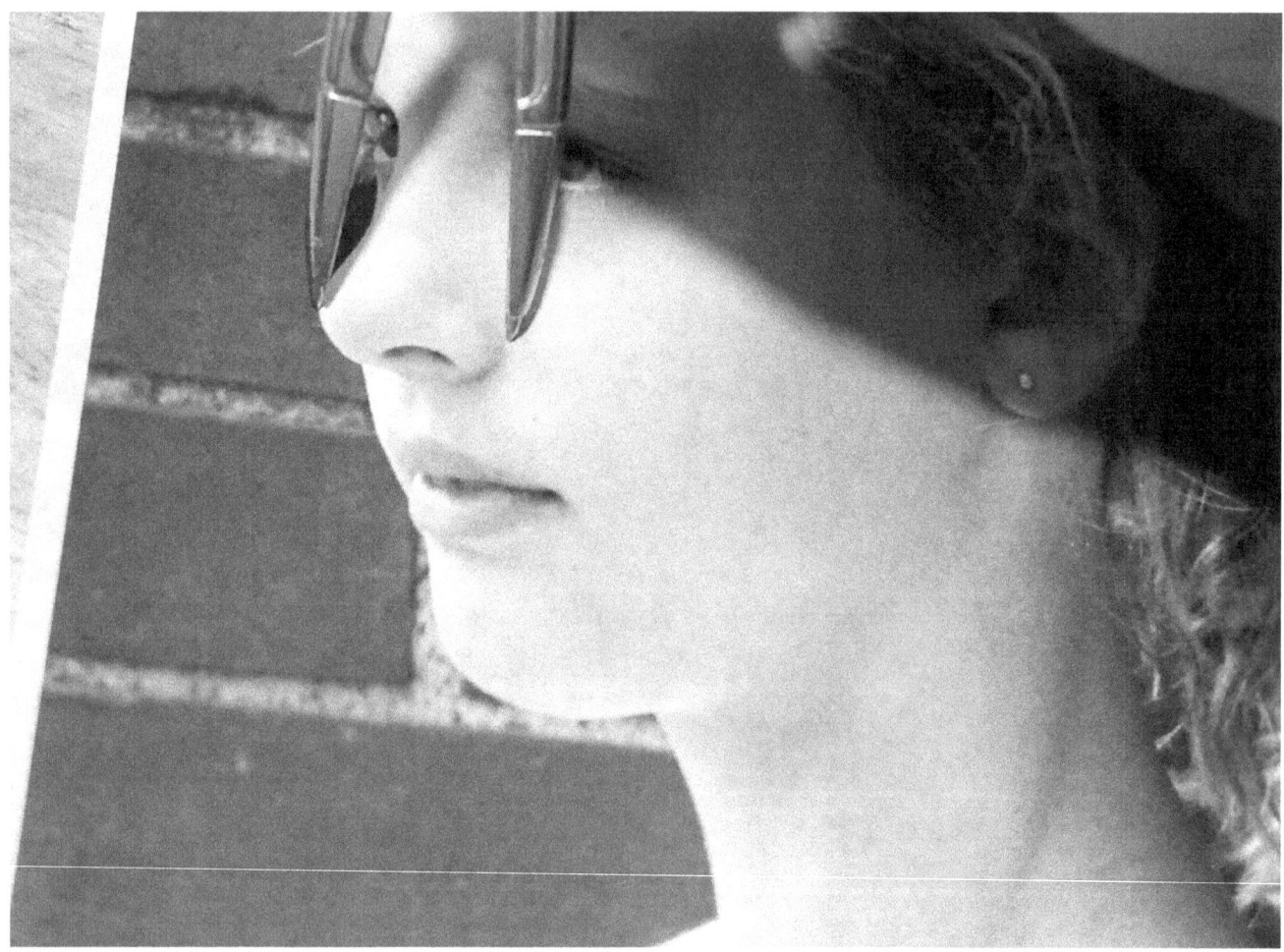

Photo C.

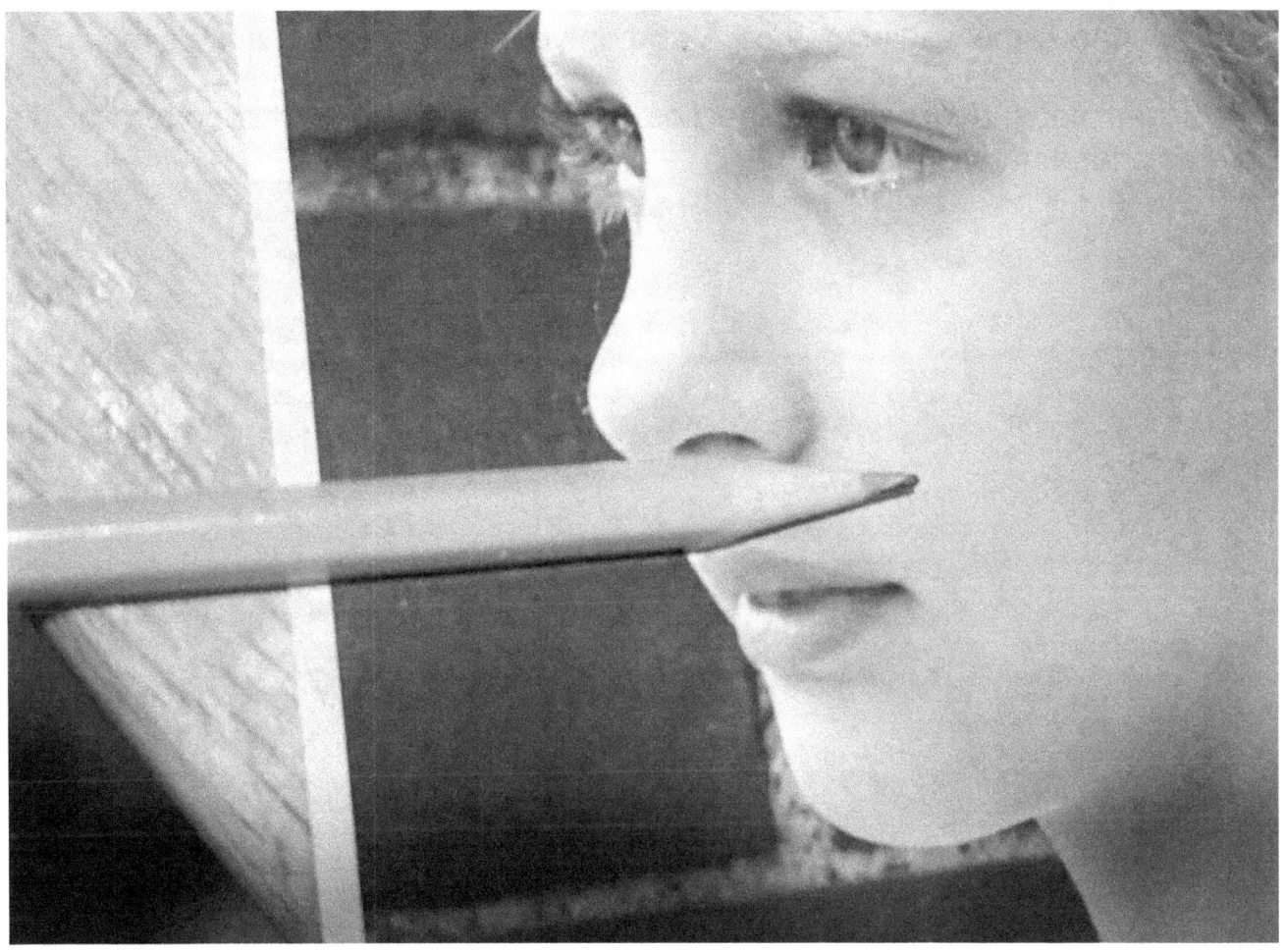

There are many methods to use for measuring a portrait but these are the three most common method that I have been using over 35 years as free hand, and it helps me to draw from real life or photograph.

I am using the photograph just to show the measurement and the way I do it. We will begin with the method A which is excellent for a beginner to learn and understand the feeling of the size. The other two methods as in B and C you can follow the same way in method A and on your own, and it is quite simple.

Here I am measuring between the lips in the groove up to the bottom of the nose as a landmark.

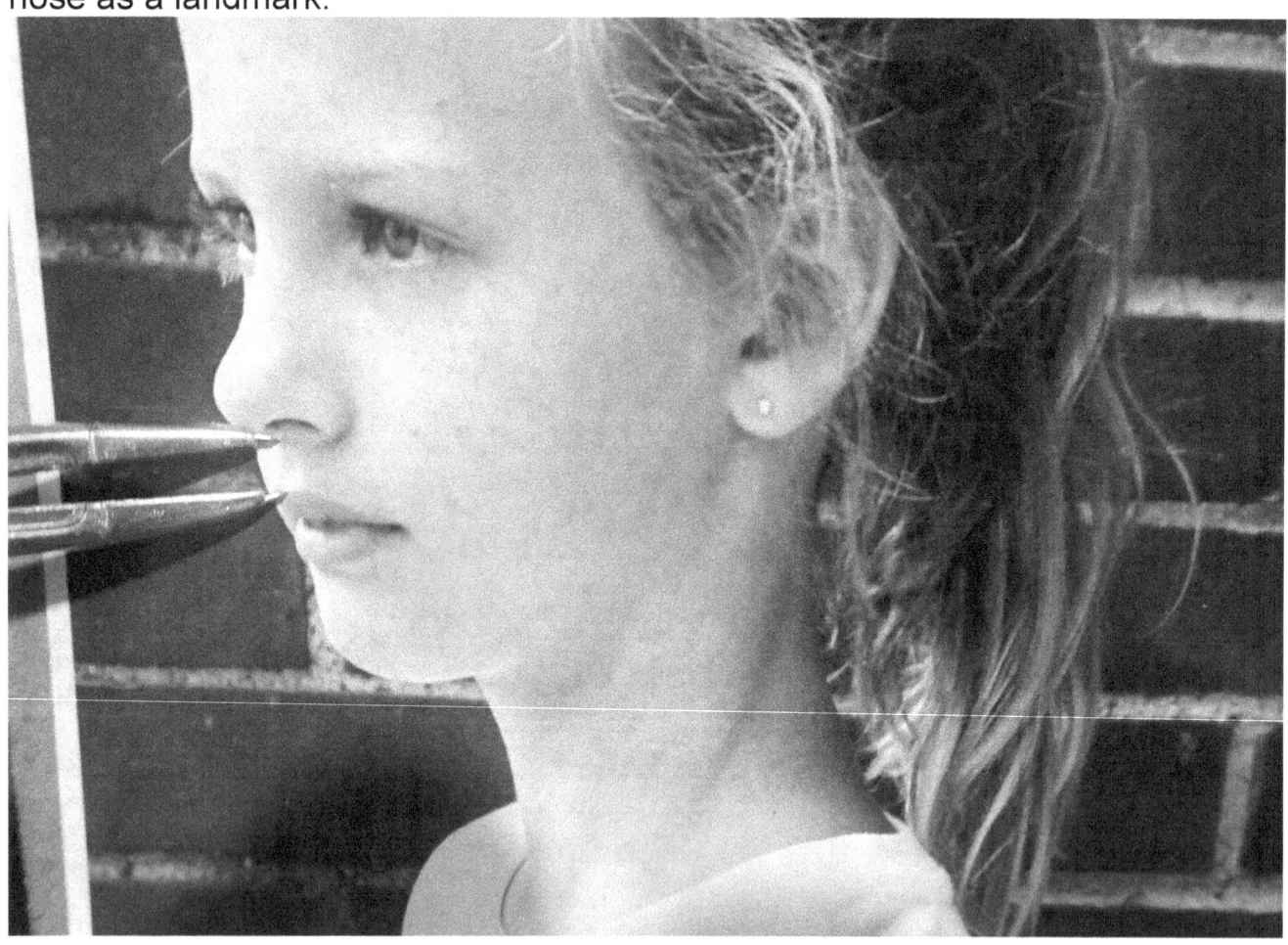

Keep in mind, I always work my drawing from the inside and going outward while making the portrait. Here below, I keep measuring upward toward the eyebrows and stop there. For her portrait, there are five spaces from the bottom of the nose to the line of the eyebrows. That will become a measurement to center the portrait on the paper. See the next page on 20.

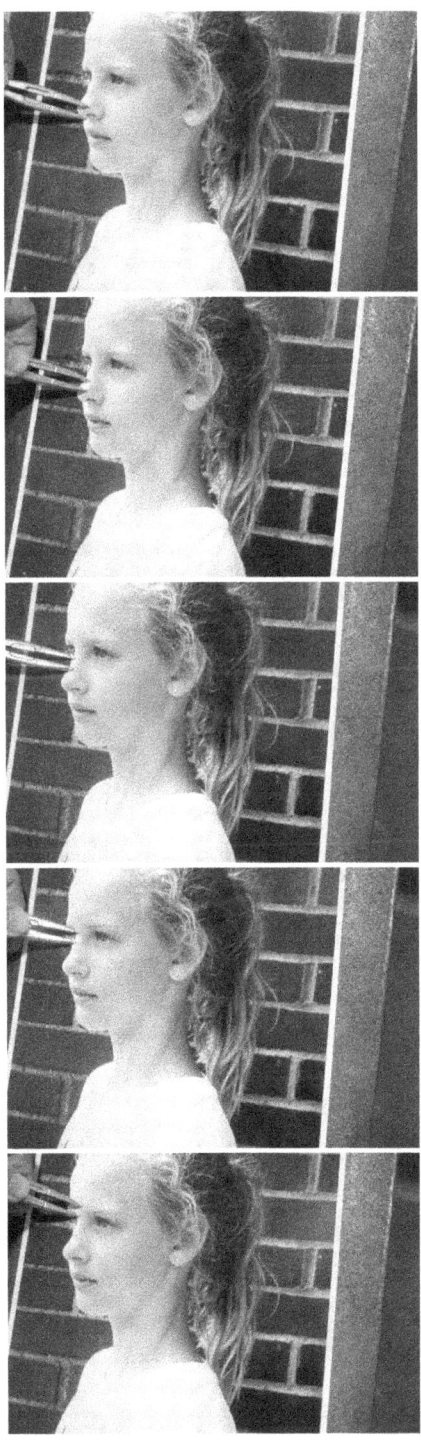

In the first center photo, I am using the nose measurement to center the portrait on the paper. Then I would use this measurement for the top to bottom shown in the last four photos then transfer over to the drawing paper to make sure it fits in.

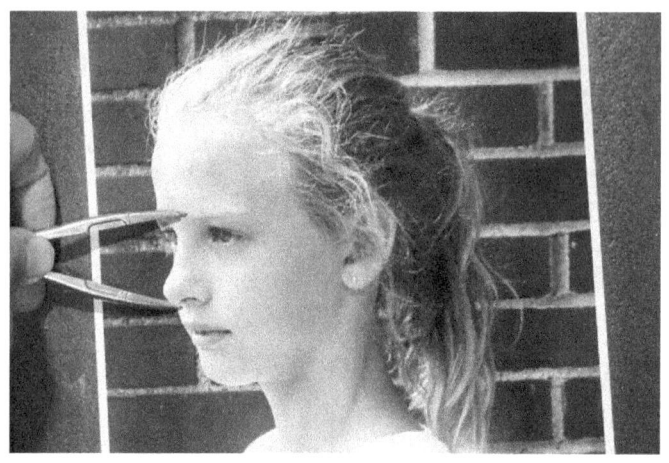

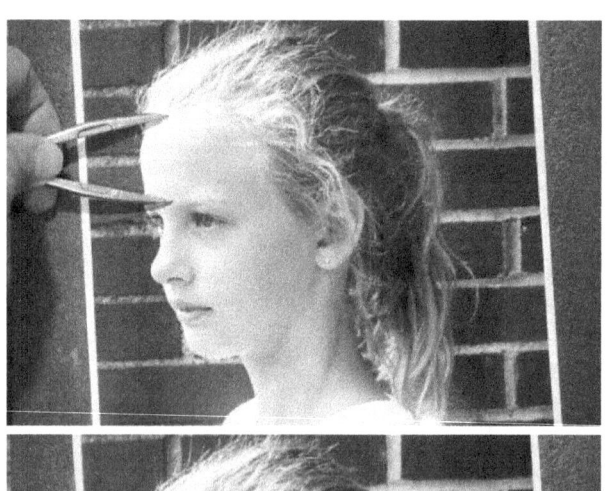

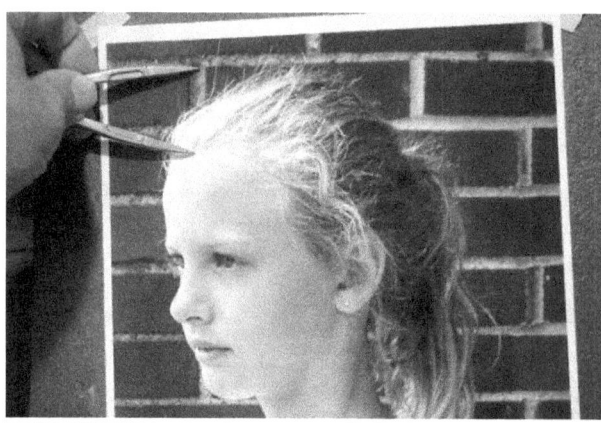

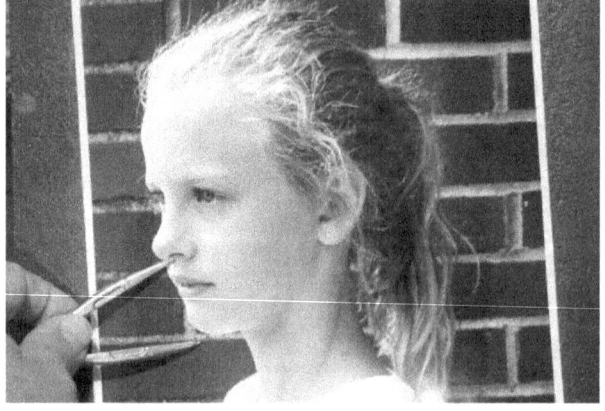

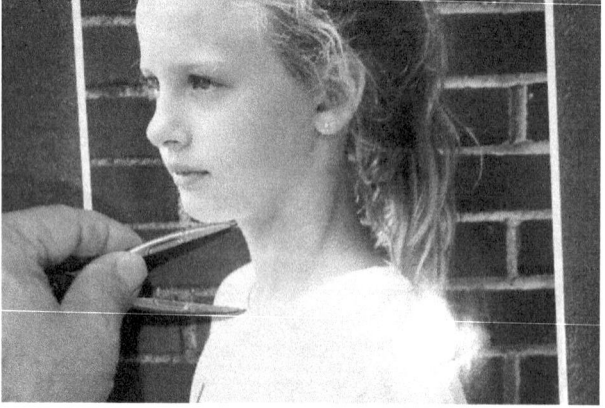

Then I would measure from side to side to make sure it fits inside the drawing paper. Remember that method in photo A on page 15 is the foundation for this drawing and it would be the center of the attention. It depends how big your paper is and how big your portrait will be. Play around with it freely until you are comfortable with the position of the face on the drawing paper.

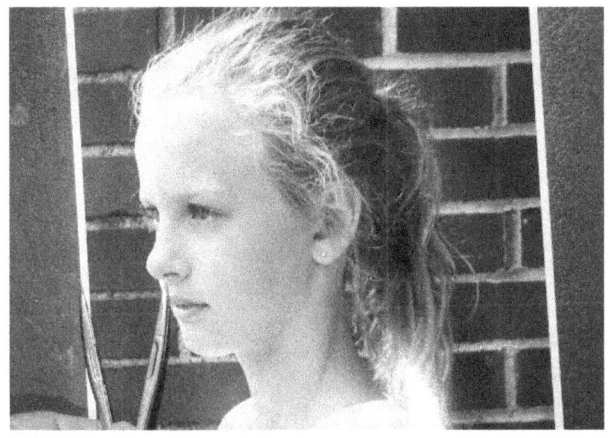
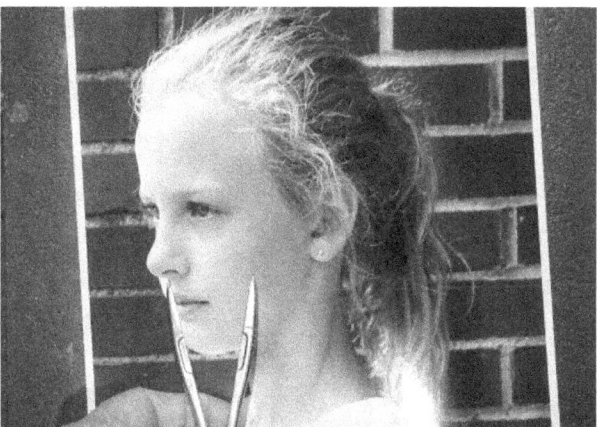
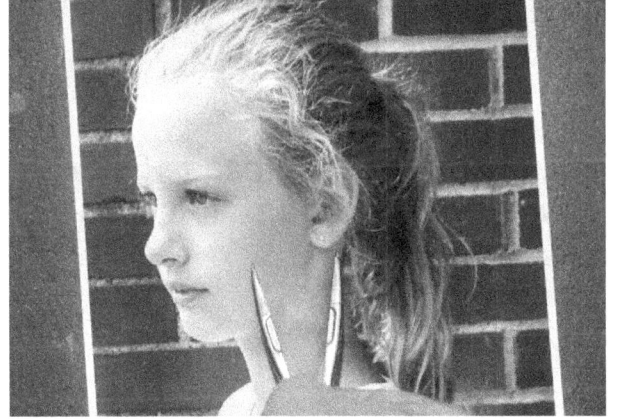
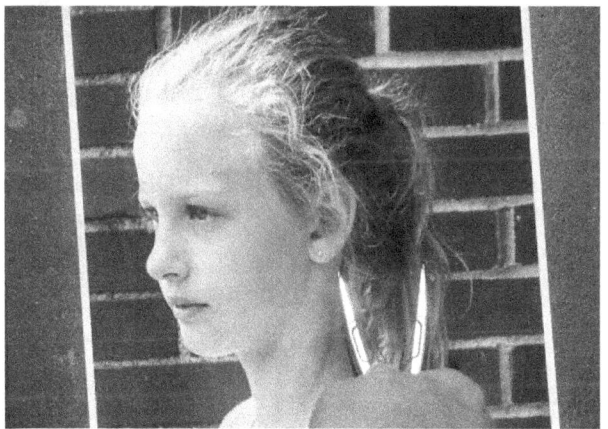

Here is the Bristol drawing paper on masonite board with masking tape on four corners.

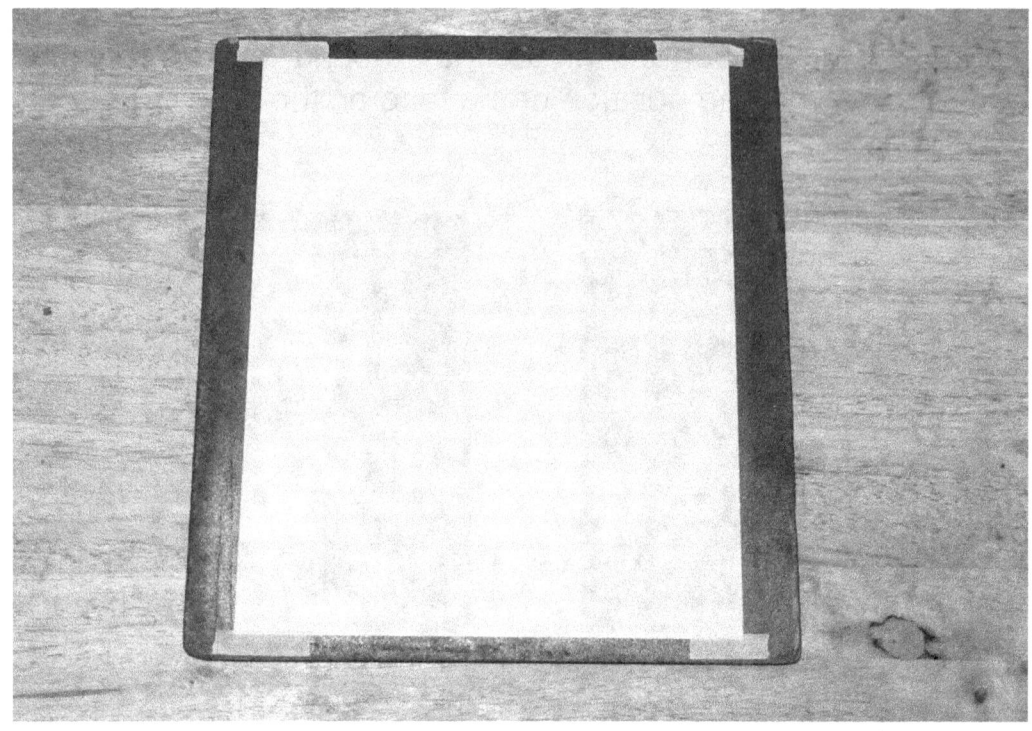

There, I made a ballpark of where the method in Photo A (page 15) measurement would be by using the compass with a pencil and start marking it, see below.

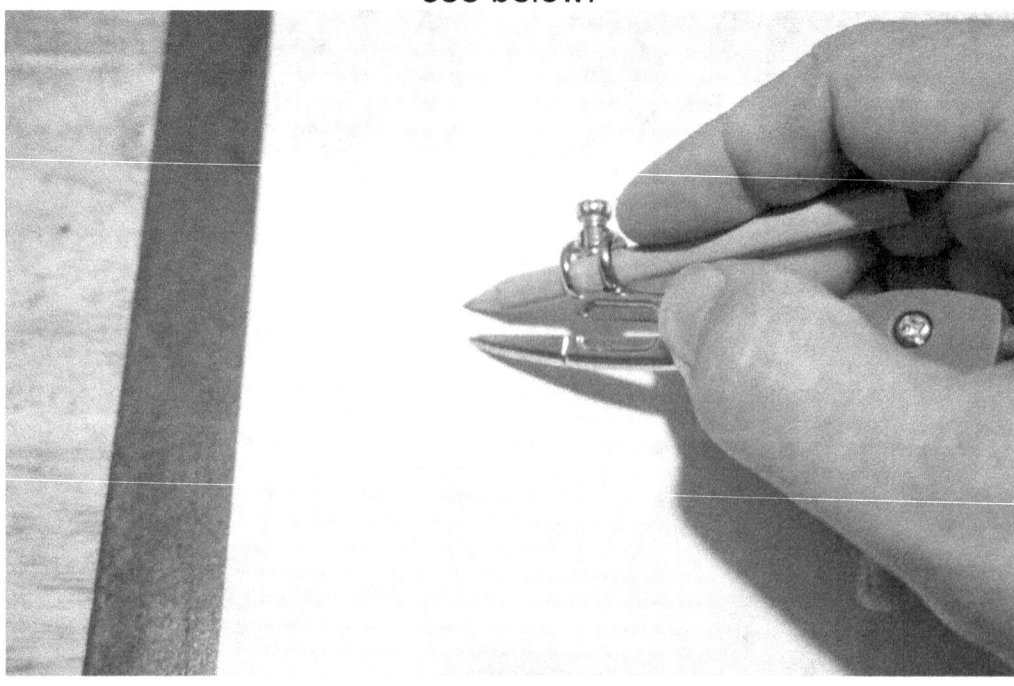

Here I start marking five spaces for the nose plus one space below the nose to the lips, the Method A.

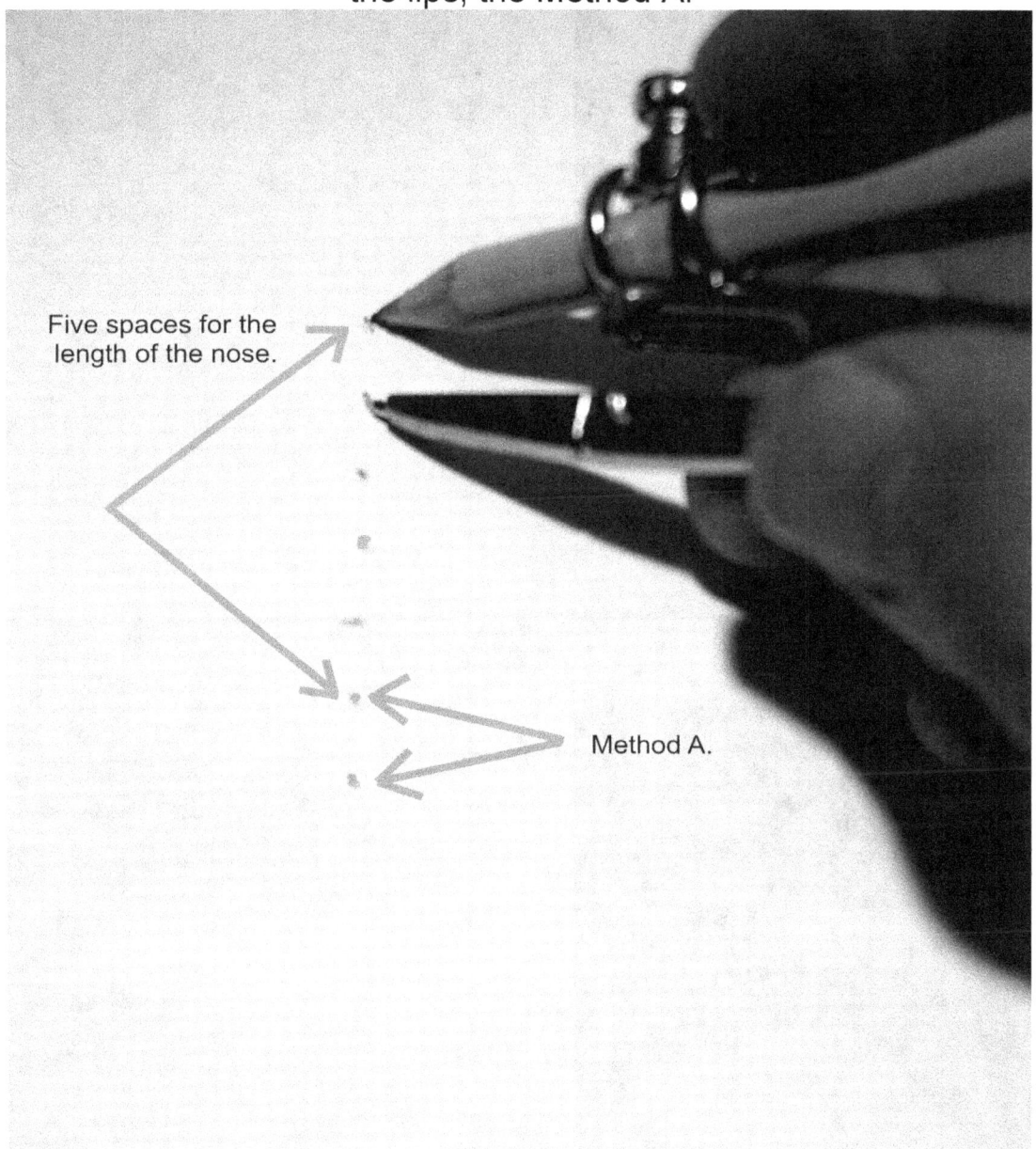

Five spaces for the length of the nose.

Method A.

Before I continue the measuring, I will go back to make sure the portrait is line up or fit in from the nose measurement, the five spaces on page 23 by using the analysis on page 20 and 21. It is critical to do this since you may not want the portrait to be going off the paper.

In the next few pages, we are going to measure the rest of the face in an up and down position which is the central axis. Follow the numbers as step by step.

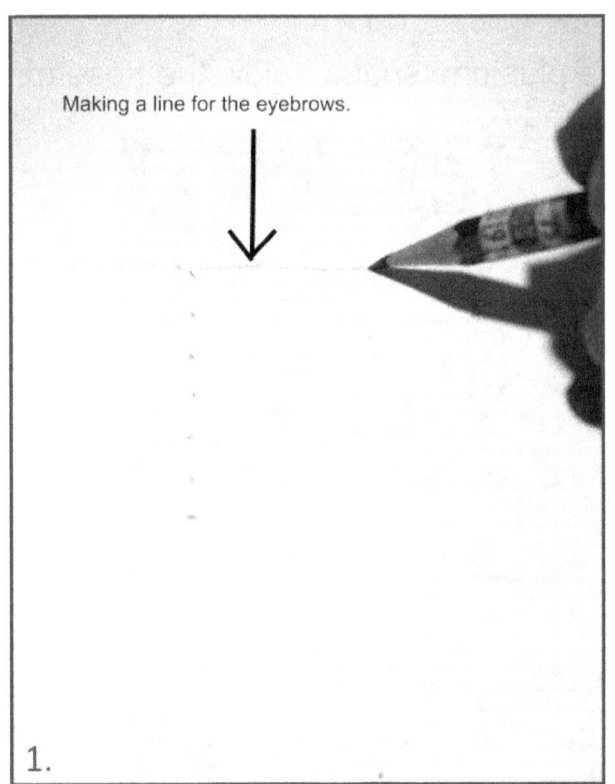

Making a line for the eyebrows.

1.

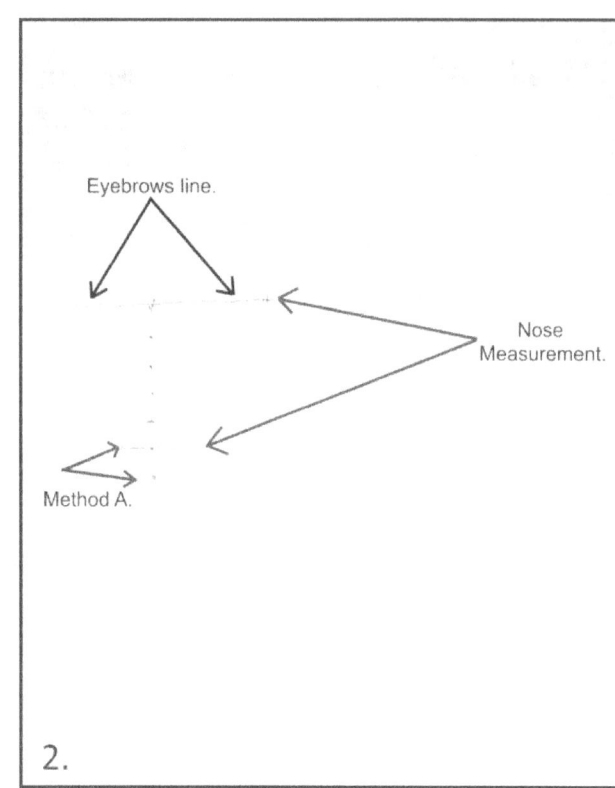

Eyebrows line.

Nose
Measurement.

Method A.

2.

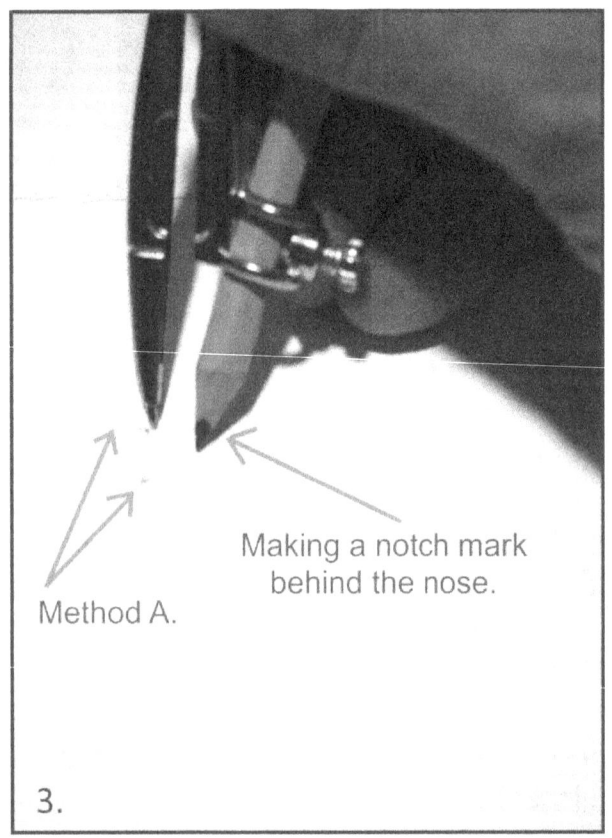

Method A.

Making a notch mark
behind the nose.

3.

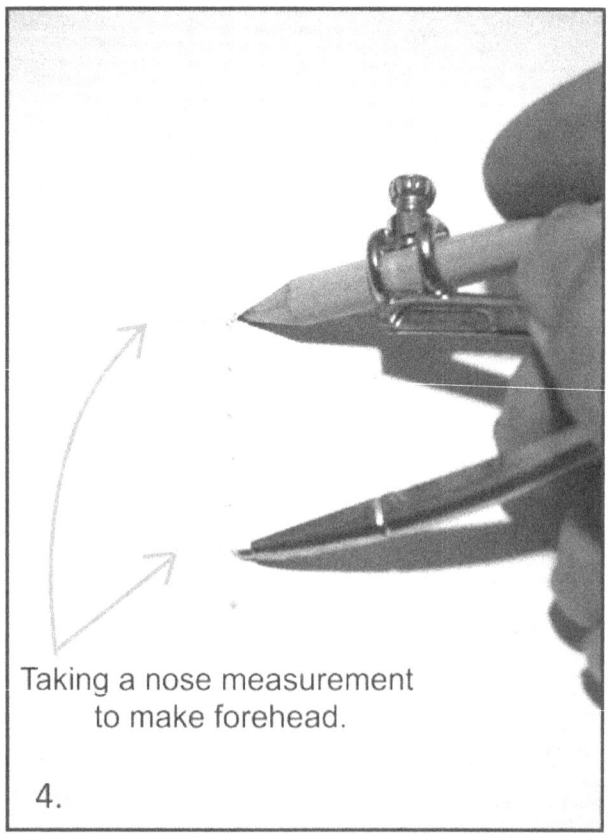

Taking a nose measurement
to make forehead.

4.

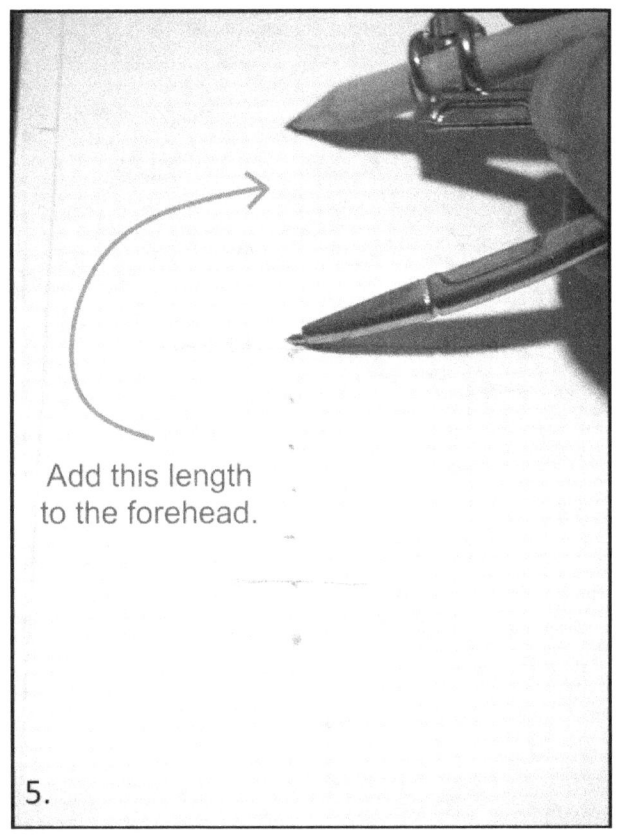

Add this length to the forehead.

5.

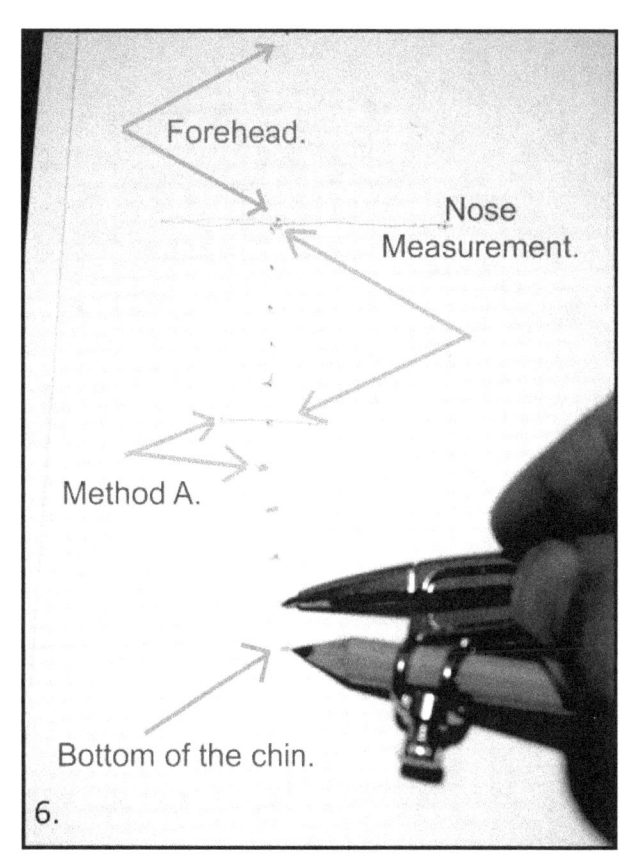

Forehead.

Nose Measurement.

Method A.

Bottom of the chin.

6.

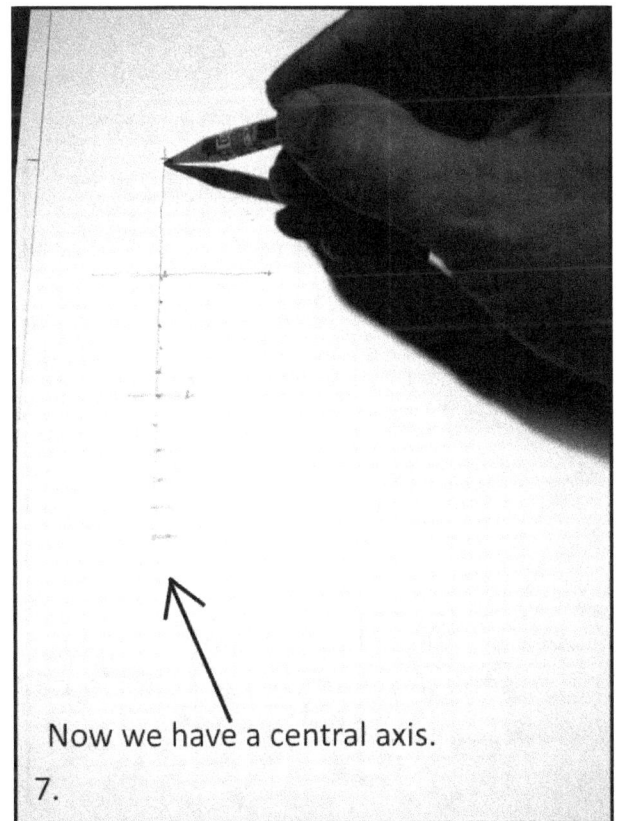

Now we have a central axis.

7.

Go to the next page for a complete measurement.

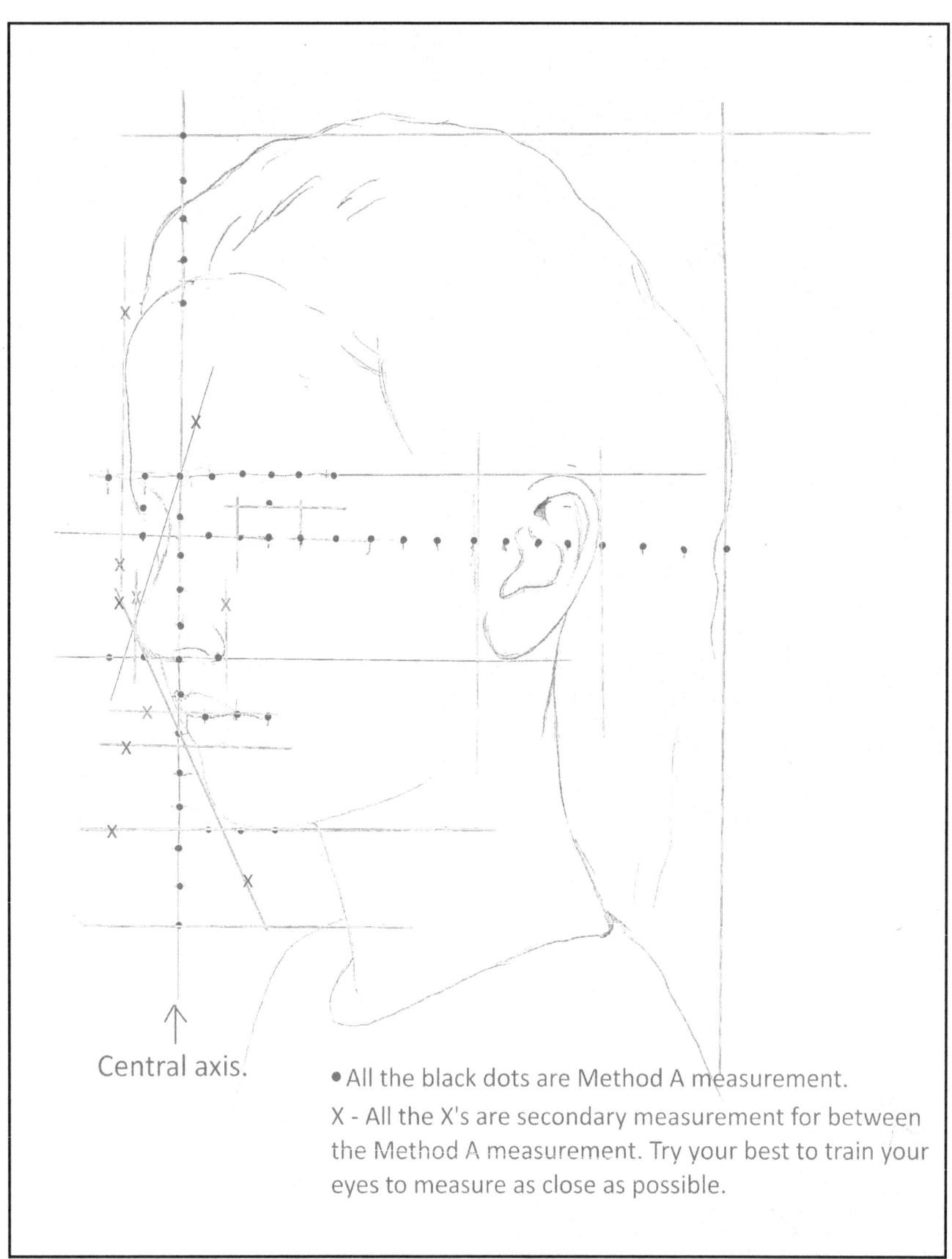

↑
Central axis.

• All the black dots are Method A measurement.

X - All the X's are secondary measurement for between the Method A measurement. Try your best to train your eyes to measure as close as possible.

Fourth Chapter
Diagrams-Worksheets

I added several different beginners to advanced worksheets. The goal is to practice and finish the drawing in the draft. It does not have to be perfect. You want to get a sense and the feel of the subject with the methods I have shared with you in this book.

Please make many copies on thick, smooth paper of these diagrams-worksheets for practice so you can save these original diagrams-worksheets for later use.

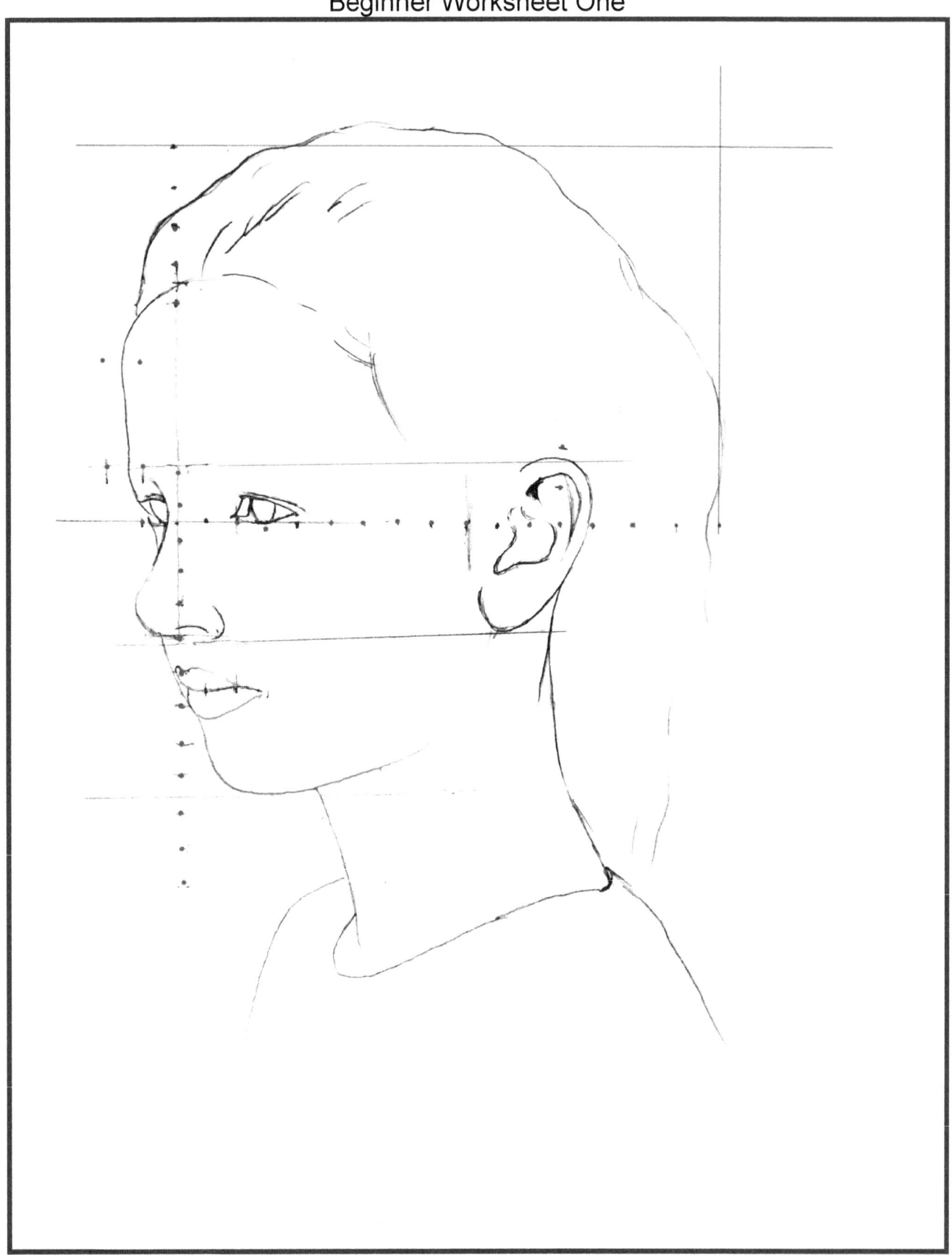

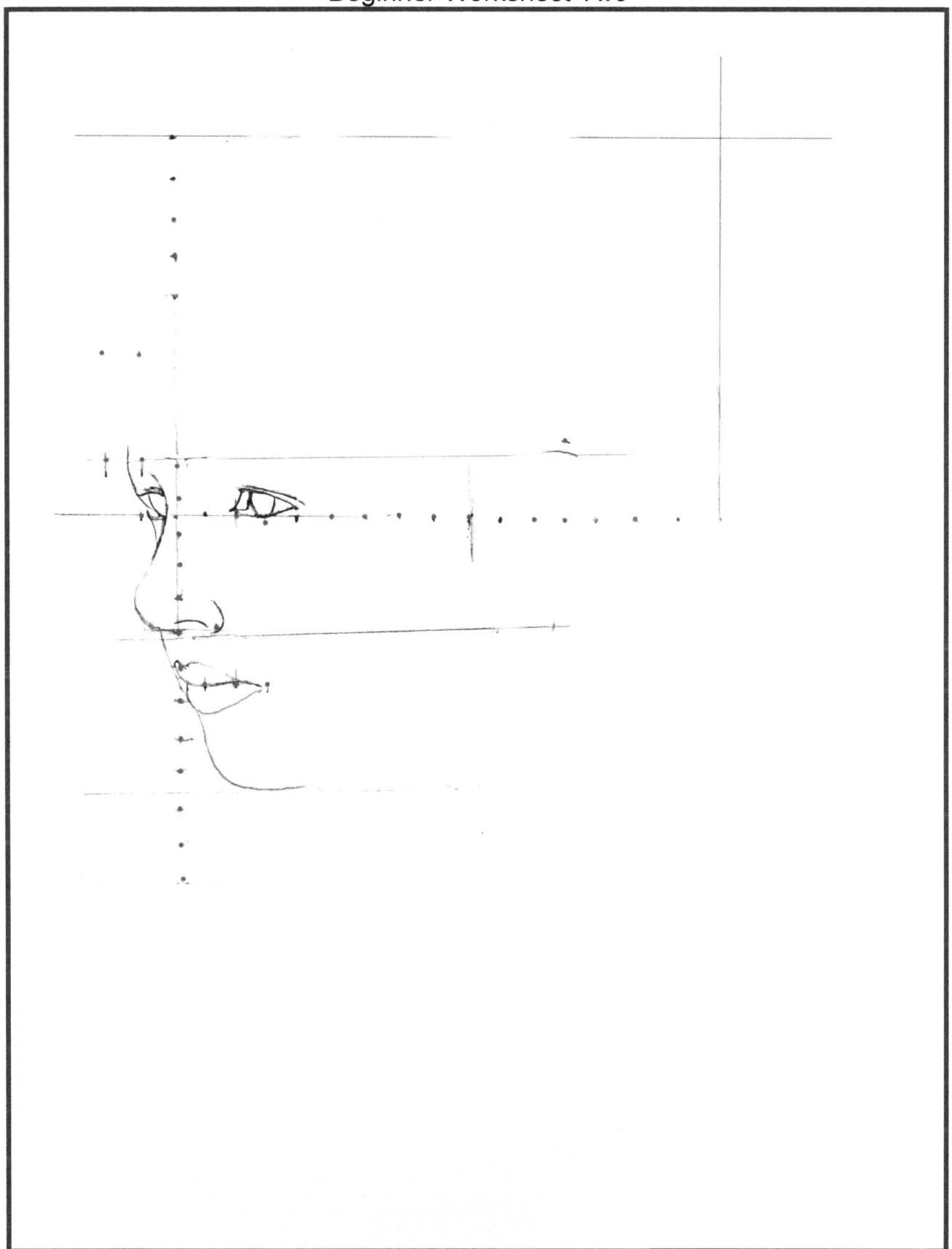

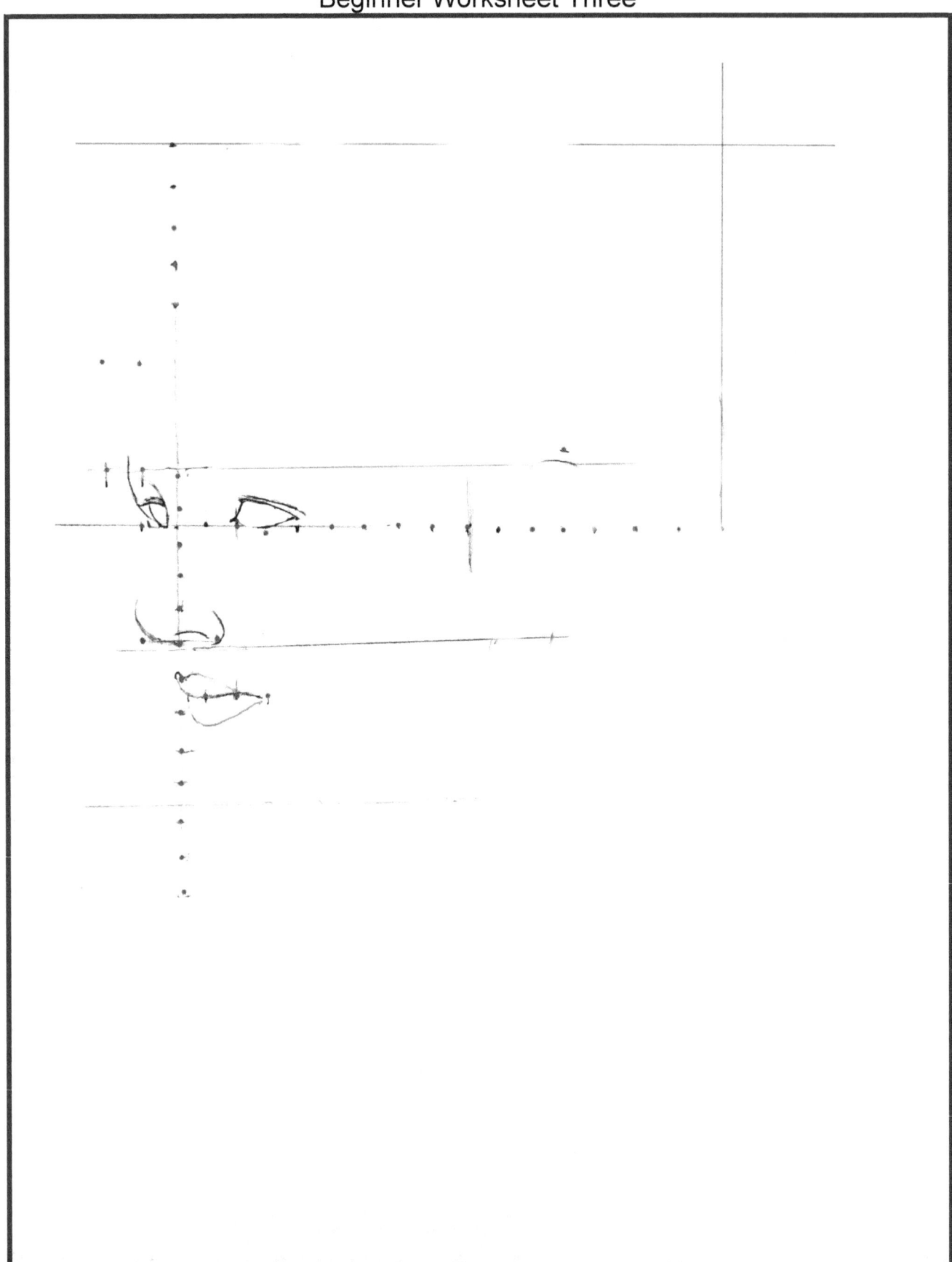

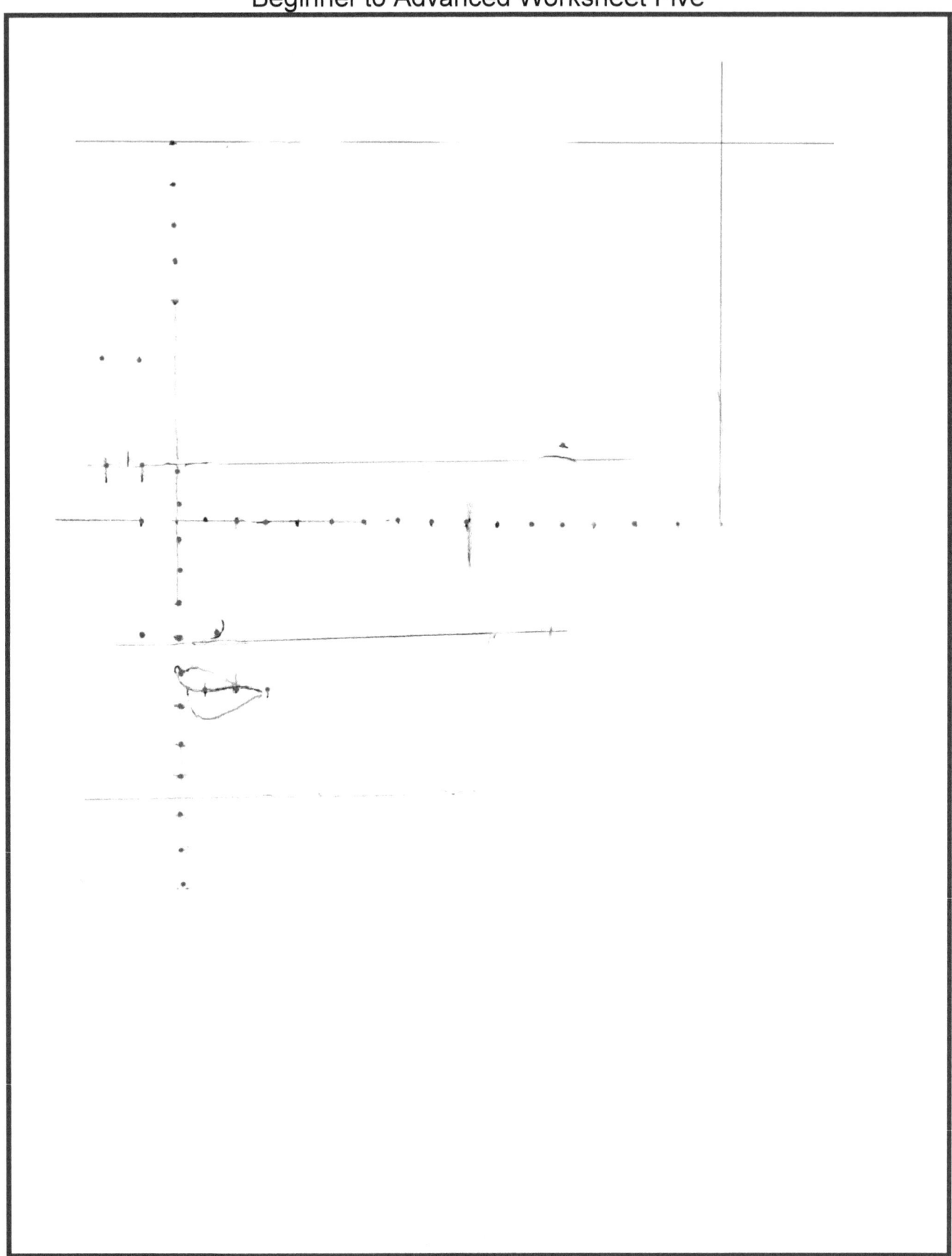

Advanced Worksheet Eight
You can start using on drawing paper instead on this actual diagram.
Make sure it is in the same position as this diagram.

Fifth Chapter
Drawing Techniques

Here are some of the drawing techniques in the pictures that I use for most of my drawing and it is done on my favorite paper called Bristol because these type of paper allow me to move the shade smoothly with a pure stroke and at the same time it allows me to rub the pencil in hard to get the shade I want. It's a tough and a very smooth paper all around to work with for me.

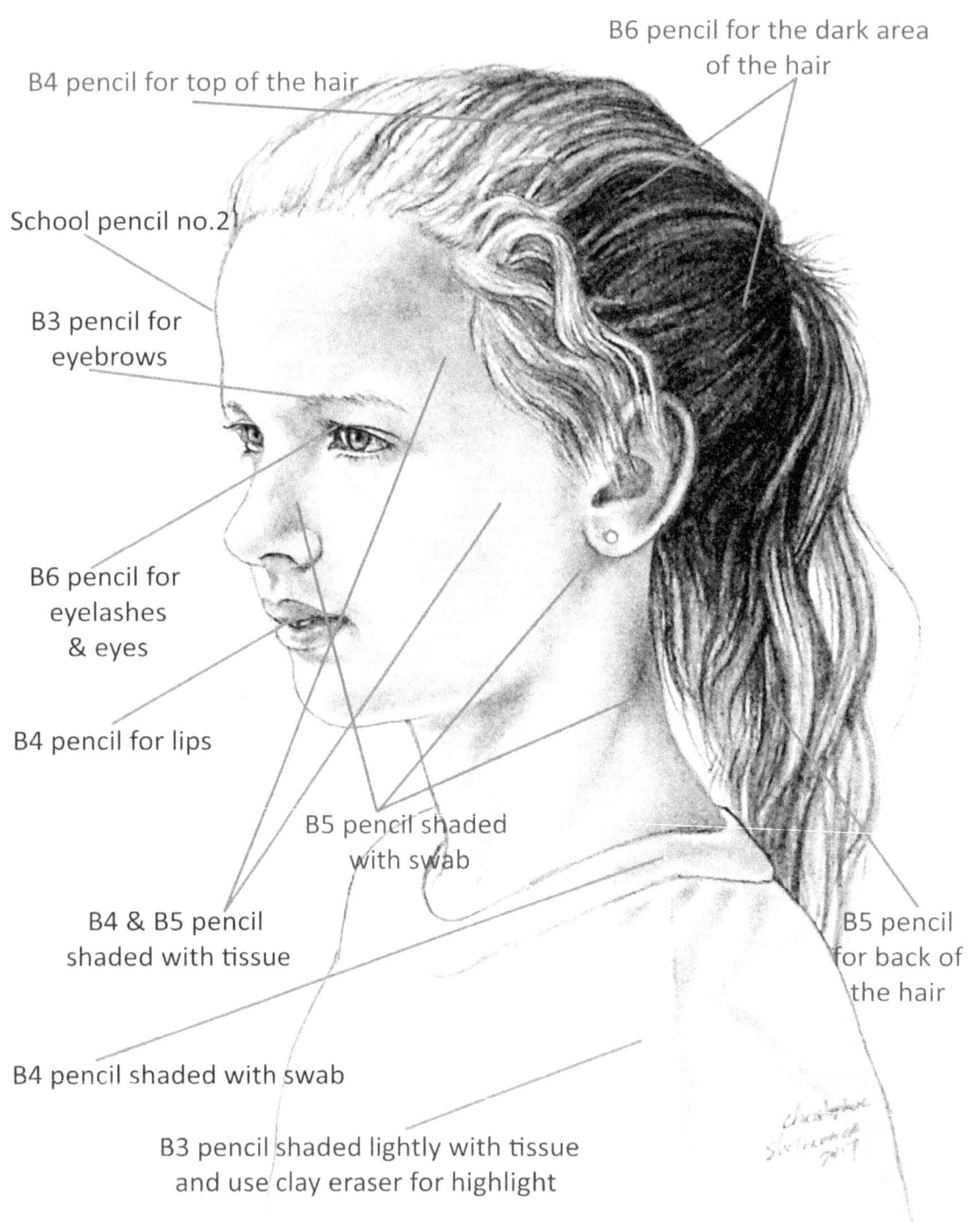

B6 pencil for the dark area of the hair

B4 pencil for top of the hair

School pencil no.2

B3 pencil for eyebrows

B6 pencil for eyelashes & eyes

B4 pencil for lips

B5 pencil shaded with swab

B4 & B5 pencil shaded with tissue

B5 pencil for back of the hair

B4 pencil shaded with swab

B3 pencil shaded lightly with tissue and use clay eraser for highlight

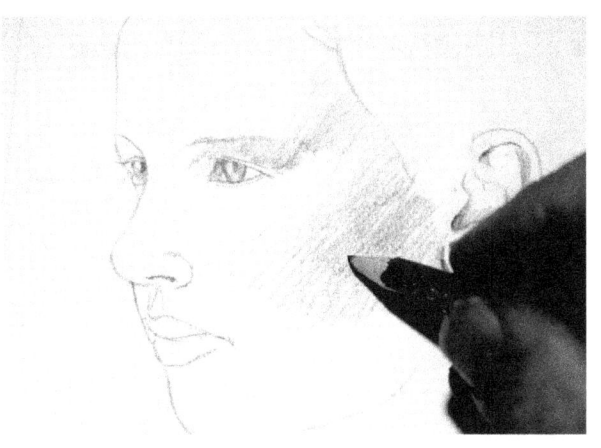 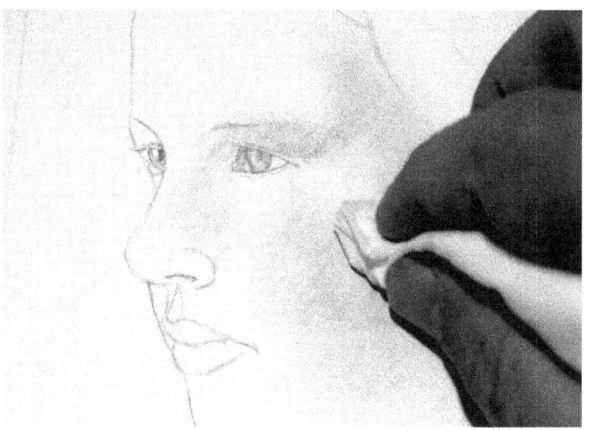

Here, first I draw or shaded lightly with B4 and B5 pencils. Then I rub it in with the white tissue for the cheeks and use a cotton swab for the smaller area as the nose, under the chin, on the side of the forehead, back of the neck and the ear.

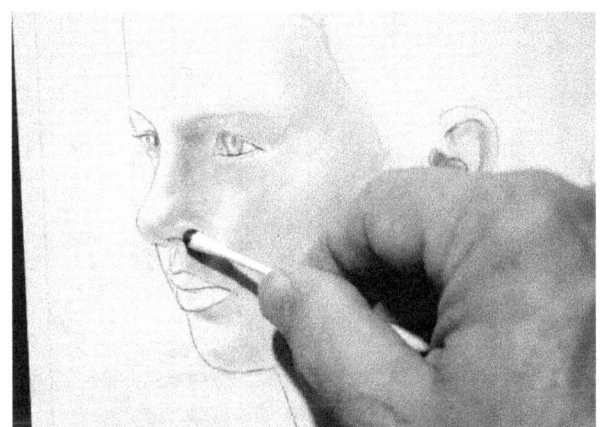 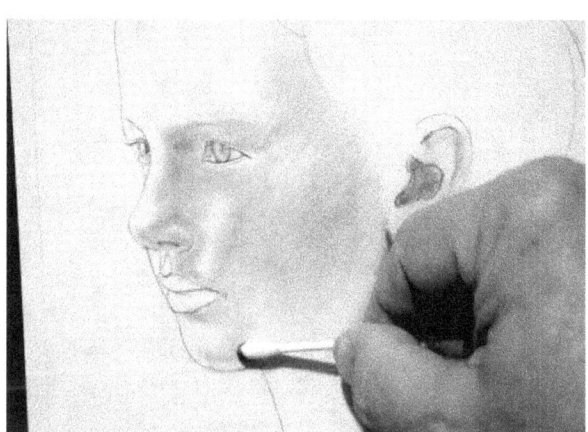

For now, we have to an end, and in the hope, this is the beginning of your new knowledge and more skills from learning this book. I hope this will improve and help your skills to go the next level of your goal and I thank you for your interest and support for this drawing project.

Peace, Christopher Shellhammer

For my special and caring friends, Terry and Camp.

Biography:

Award winning American Artist Christopher Shellhammer's work has been exhibited in galleries and exhibitions for over thirty-five years and viewed online from around the world since 2003. His works have been collected and supported by hundreds of art collectors. Alongside his art career, he has been writing poems, thoughts, and short stories. More about the author/artist can be viewed at www.christophershellhammergallery.com

www.ingramcontent.com/pod-product-compliance
Lightning Source LLC
Chambersburg PA
CBHW081237170526
45165CB00009B/3080